The Library of the Middle Ages™

Saladin and the Kingdom of Jerusalem

The Muslims Recapture the Holy Land in AD 1187

Lee Hancock

rosen
central™

The Rosen Publishing Group, Inc., New York

Published in 2004 by The Rosen Publishing Group, Inc.
29 East 21st Street, New York, NY 10010

Library of Congress Cataloging-in-Publication Data

Hancock, Lee.
Saladin and the Kingdom of Jerusalem: the Muslims recapture the Holy Land in AD 1187/Lee Hancock.—1st ed.
    p. cm.—(The library of the Middle Ages)
Includes bibliographical references and index.
ISBN 0-8239-4217-1 (lib. bdg.)
1. Saladin, Sultan of Egypt and Syria, 1137–1193—Juvenile literature. 2. Crusades—Juvenile literature. 3. Jerusalem—History—Latin Kingdom, 1099–1244—Juvenile literature. 4. Christianity—Relations—Islam—History—To 1500—Juvenile literature. 5. Islam—Relations—Christianity—History—To 1500—Juvenile literature.
I. Title: Saladin and the Kingdom of Jerusalem.
II. Title: Saladin and the Kingdom of Jerusalem.
III. Title. IV. Series.

DS38.4.S2H36 2003
956'.014—dc21
                                        2003001188

Manufactured in the United States of America

Table of Contents

1 The Latin Kingdom of Jerusalem 5

2 Saladin 23

3 The Recapture of Jerusalem 31

4 The Return of the Crusaders 47

Glossary 55

For More Information 57

For Further Reading 59

Bibliography 61

Index 62

A battle between crusaders and Muslim warriors, from a fourteenth-century French manuscript illumination

The Latin Kingdom of Jerusalem

hen Pope Urban II made his famous speech at Clermont, France, in November 1095, calling on Christians to go to the Holy Land and reclaim it from the Muslims, he cannot have known that his words would set in motion a series of events that would have such far-reaching consequences. Urban's speech started the age of the Crusades, which would last for almost two hundred years and would result in much death and bloodshed. Before we can look at why this happened, and see how Saladin and the Kingdom of Jerusalem fit into the picture, we need to look at the events leading up to Urban's speech and why he felt that he had to make it.

At the beginning of the seventh century AD, the people of the Middle East were mainly Christian. But a new and dynamic force, Islam, beginning to come out of Arabia, would seek to take over the lands of the Christians. By the time of the death of the new religion's founder, Muhammad, in 632, most of the Middle East was in Muslim hands. The city of Jerusalem was taken over by the Muslims in 638. Jerusalem was looked upon as a holy city by both Christians and Muslims. The Muslims believed that Muhammad had risen to heaven from Jerusalem, and to mark the spot where they believed this happened, they built a large mosque called the Dome of the Rock. For the Christians, Jerusalem was of great significance because the city was where Jesus had lived and where most of the later events of the New Testament had taken place, including Jesus' crucifixion. To mark the place where Jesus was supposed to have been buried, Christians built a special monument, the Church of the Holy Sepulchre.

Although Jerusalem was now an Islamic city, the Muslims still allowed Christians to visit the city on pilgrimages. But in the middle of the eleventh century, the Arabs were replaced as the leaders of the Muslims by the Turks, who weren't as accepting of the Christians as the Arabs had been. The pilgrims began to be attacked by the Turks. Out of fears for their safety, most Christians only went to the Holy Land if they were in large, armed groups. The Turks were also fighting a war against the Christians of the Byzantine Empire, and the Byzantine emperor, Alexius I, appealed to Urban for help in the war against the Muslims.

This was the background to Pope Urban's call for Christian expeditions to the East, not only to aid Emperor Alexius and protect the pilgrims but to recapture the Holy Lands, and Jerusalem especially, from the Muslims. Around thirty thousand people responded to the pope's message, and this army, mainly made up of French nobles, set out in the summer of 1096 to invade the East. This was the beginning of what was called the First Crusade. The crusaders fought hard and bloody battles against the Turks, and by 1099 they

A twelfth-century Italian manuscript depicts a crusader and a Moor in combat. The Moors were Muslims from North Africa who invaded Spain in the eighth century.

had finally reached Jerusalem. After a five-week siege, they entered Jerusalem on July 15, and to celebrate their victory the crusaders went on a murderous rampage, massacring their Muslim enemies.

With Jerusalem now back in Christian hands, the crusaders began to build up a new group of states in the area that they called Outremer, which means "across the sea" in the old French language. Outremer was made up of four separate states: the County of Edessa, the Principality of Antioch, the County of Tripoli, and most important of all, the Kingdom of Jerusalem. Although the Christians had won back the city, the Muslims still regarded Jerusalem as one of their holy cities, and it would be only a matter of time before they tried to recapture it. The crusaders were safe for the moment because the Muslims were fighting among themselves and no leader had emerged who could unify the Islamic world and focus its energies on the Christian invaders. But as we shall see, one man did bring all the separate strands of the Muslim world together, and his name was Saladin.

Most of the crusaders who captured Jerusalem decided to go back to their homes. They had achieved what they set out to do—recapture the city—and felt that their work was done. Those who stayed on to build up the Outremer states faced a number of serious problems. The region that the crusaders had decided to call home was essentially a narrow strip of land between the Mediterranean Sea and the Syrian Desert. The climate and terrain were totally different from the European landscape that the crusaders were used to. And the newly Christianized city was like a small island in an Islamic sea. Although the Muslims were not united at this time, the surrounding Muslim lands still posed a considerable threat to the crusaders. Around three thousand crusaders remained in Jerusalem after the taking of the city in 1099 to establish this new kingdom, but by the following spring it was said that only two hundred knights and one thousand civilians remained. When you look at the dangers and hardships that the new inhabitants faced, it is not surprising that most of the crusaders had gone back to Europe.

Jerusalem came to be known as the "Latin" Kingdom of Jerusalem, and the population was referred to as Latins because its people were members of the Roman Catholic

Crusaders disembark in the Holy Land and enter a fortified city in this illustration from a fifteenth-century French manuscript.

Church, in which Latin was the language used in church services and prayer. For general day-to-day use, however, French was spoken, as most of the crusaders had come from this part of Europe, including the man who became the leader of the new kingdom, Godfrey of Bouillon. Born

The old city of Jerusalem, showing the Lion Gate, also known as St. Stephen's Gate

around 1058, he was a fairly important lord from northern France, although it appears that he was not too wealthy. To finance his journey on the Crusade, he had to mortgage all of his property. Despite his financial hardships, Godfrey became one of the leaders of the First Crusade, and it was his army that was the first to break through the wall of Jerusalem during the battle for the city. One week after the capture of the city, Godfrey was offered the kingship of Jerusalem, but declined this invitation, instead calling himself Advocatus Sancti Sepulchri, Latin for "Advocate of the Holy Sepulchre."

Under the new Latin rulers, Jerusalem's architecture and culture started to once again take on a more Westernized Christian character. One of the main reasons for the First Crusade was the recapture of the Church of the Holy Sepulchre, erected upon what was believed to be Jesus' burial place. The church had originally been built by the Byzantine Empire, but attacks on the empire, and thus the church, had seen its almost complete destruction by 1009. The Byzantine emperor, Constantine IX, had started renovation on the church in 1030. When the crusaders conquered the city, they carried on the church's restoration. The Latins actually reduced the size of the church by building a large convent where the original Byzantine basilica had been. But the task of rebuilding such an important monument was still a mammoth job, and work wasn't completed until 1149.

The Latins also went on to build or restore many more churches in the city and the surrounding area. One of the finest churches to have been built was the Church of St. Anne, named after the mother of the Virgin Mary. Another impressive structure was the Church of St. Mary of the Germans, erected in the first half of the twelfth century. Originally intended to be a center for the German knights and pilgrims who came to the city, the church was just one part of a large collection of buildings called the Teutonic Complex. As well as the church, the complex included a two-storied structure that had a hospital on the upper level and a ceremonial hall on the ground floor.

Life in Jerusalem

The Latins never forgot that there was still a danger from the surrounding Muslims, so the city's defenses and fortifications had to be able to withstand an attack. There were the remains of an old citadel (a fortress) that housed a large tower, the Tower of David, at the western wall of the city. These existing defenses were, however, in an extremely weak state, so to keep the city safe, the citadel and the tower had to undergo massive reconstruction. The Latins rebuilt the citadel and doubled its original size, also putting a moat around it for extra safety. They enlarged the citadel because, with the growing population of Jerusalem, the people needed shelter in case of an attack by the Muslims. As the citadel was now so strong, it was hoped that the Latins could remain there in safety until reinforcements arrived.

Before the crusaders captured Jerusalem, the Muslims had destroyed all the agricultural resources around the city. They did this so that the crusaders would not be able to advance quickly because food supplies would not be available for their army. Because of this, when the crusaders did capture the city, they had to resettle the area and build more

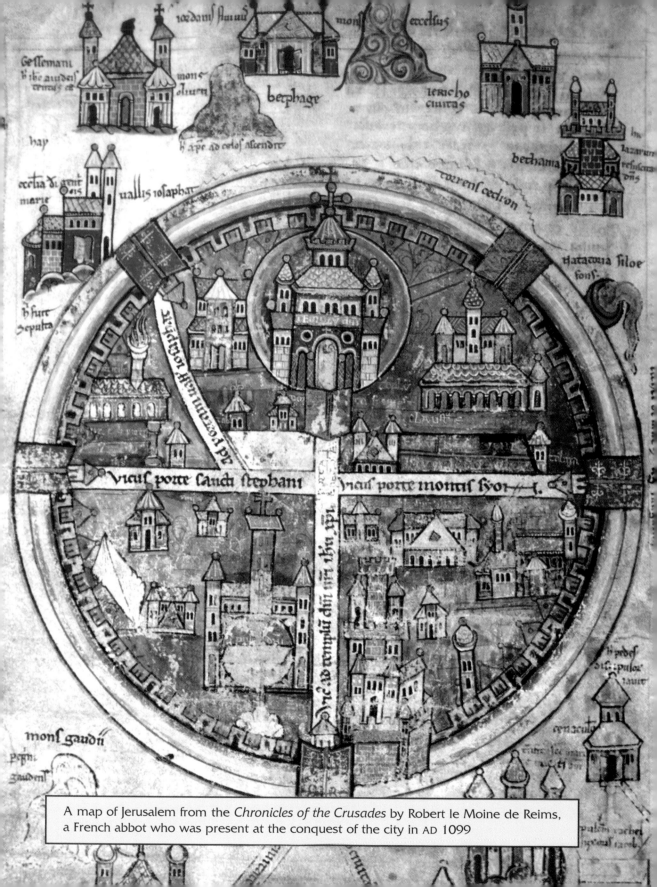

A map of Jerusalem from the *Chronicles of the Crusades* by Robert le Moine de Reims, a French abbot who was present at the conquest of the city in AD 1099

farms in the region to supply food and wine for the new population. It also meant that the Latins had to trade with the local Muslims if they were to survive. One of the first steps Godfrey had taken after capturing Jerusalem was to try to gain control of all the local seaports. This would not only make it easier for supplies from Europe to enter the kingdom, but it would also mean that Godfrey would have control of all the local trade routes.

The local port of Jaffa was already a part of the Kingdom of Jerusalem, and Godfrey fortified this port to make it more secure for the Latins. He also managed to capture Arsuf, a town forty miles north of Jerusalem. The Muslims now realized that they would have to put aside some of their differences with the new invaders if they wished to carry on trading their goods, and many of the surrounding Muslim leaders made trade agreements with Jerusalem. This meant that traders from Jerusalem were free to go to surrounding areas to sell their goods and that Islamic merchants could come to the city to trade with the Latins.

To accommodate the city's blossoming business enterprises, the crusaders built a series of market complexes within the walls of Jerusalem. The Central Market was where the Assyrian and Latin money changers did their trade. It was also the home of the city's restaurants. Since this area was known by the locals as Malquisinat, French for "the street of bad cookery," it seems that the food served there was not to everybody's liking. West of the Central Market were the spice and vegetable markets, and to the east was the Vaulted Market, which mainly sold textiles. Other markets sold poultry, grain, and cattle.

A naval battle between the Venetians and the Egyptians outside the city of Jaffa sometime between the First and Second Crusades is depicted here in heroic style by the artist Santo Peranda (1566–1638).

The restaurants of the city might not have had a very good reputation, but the crusaders were now living in an area that was famous as a culinary paradise. Arabian and Egyptian cooks were much in demand in the kitchens of the Latins, teaching the newcomers the secrets of their superb dishes. It was fashionable in the East to use many spices in food, often far more than was really necessary. Because spices such as saffron were quite expensive, using many spices was a sign of a person's wealth, and the Latins also adopted this custom. Some of the most popular spices were sumac, mustard, clove, rosemary, and cinnamon, with coconut and licorice root also being used. The crusaders came to be impressed, too, by other local products, with figs, sugarcane, and citrus fruits being particular favorites.

The grapes of the region were of such excellent quality that the local wine from the Judean hills was famous in the area. To keep the wines chilled in the summer, snow was brought into the city from the distant mountains of Lebanon. Snow was also used to keep fruit juices cool, and these sherbets were an early version of what we now call sorbets. It was advisable to drink fruit juices or wines because the water was often polluted. The only way to collect potable water was by collecting and storing rainwater. To accomplish this the Latins built three reservoirs within the city: the Hamam el-Batrak, the Ancient Pool, and the Sheep Pool. There were two more pools outside of the city walls, one located near St. Stephen's Gate and one named after the nationality of its constructors, the German Pool.

Godfrey of Bouillon's term as leader of Jerusalem lasted just under a year, and he died on July 18, 1100. He was succeeded by his brother, Baldwin, who unlike Godfrey decided to accept the title of king of Jerusalem and was crowned as Baldwin I. But despite having such an impressive title, Baldwin could not rule the kingdom as he pleased. Jerusalem had many different social groups, and in some cases these groups rivaled the king in terms of power. One of these groups was made up of the nobles who had come over to the Holy Land as crusaders and stayed on to build up the new society. These men were often extremely wealthy and powerful people and did not like giving up their authority to someone like Baldwin who, despite now being called a king, was really just a noble like themselves.

The Church was another powerful section of society that was virtually independent of the king. With the building of the churches and the monasteries, the Church came to be as powerful in the East as it had been in the West. The ruler of the Church in Jerusalem, the patriarch, was the most important person in the kingdom besides the king. Some of the patriarchs, like Daimbert, the patriarch during Baldwin's time, even tried to establish a separate kingdom in Jerusalem, with the Church being the most powerful body in the land instead of the king.

Some other social groups that presented a serious obstacle to the king's leadership were the various religious orders of knights that were formed to protect the Latin states. The knights of these orders were a strange mixture of strictly religious monks and elite military fighters. Three of these groups, the Knights Templar, the Hospitallers of St. John, and the Teutonic Knights, came to Jerusalem and rapidly became another powerful and important group within the kingdom. They were totally independent of the king and the other nobles, and the only person who had any authority over them was the pope.

Despite these problems for the king, the kingdom itself was becoming increasingly rich and prosperous. The excellent trade in the area meant that Jerusalem had become one of the most wealthy and thriving states in the world. But despite all this success, the threat from its Muslim neighbors was an ever-present danger. The Turks, who the crusaders had taken Jerusalem from, began to lose their power in the Islamic world. Slowly but surely the Muslims began to regroup. They stopped fighting among themselves, and turned their attention toward their common enemy, the Christians. The Muslims decided to launch a crusade of their own, or as they called it, a *jihad*, or holy war. Where before the Muslims had lacked a single leader who could lead all the different Muslim groups, new leaders began to come forward who could unite the Islamic world.

A twelfth-century Persian bowl

One of the first of these leaders was called Zengi, who in 1144 took control of one of the original crusader states, the County of Edessa. The Christians, worried about the loss of one of their main strongholds in the East, launched the

Saladin and the Kingdom of Jerusalem

Second Crusade to try to win back the land from the Muslims. Unfortunately for the Latins, the Second Crusade was an almost total failure. With enthusiasm for crusading in the West dampened by this lack of success, the Muslims began to chip away at the other crusader states. After Zengi, other Muslim leaders took up where he had left off and claimed the leadership of the Muslim world. And the greatest of these leaders was a man called Saladin.

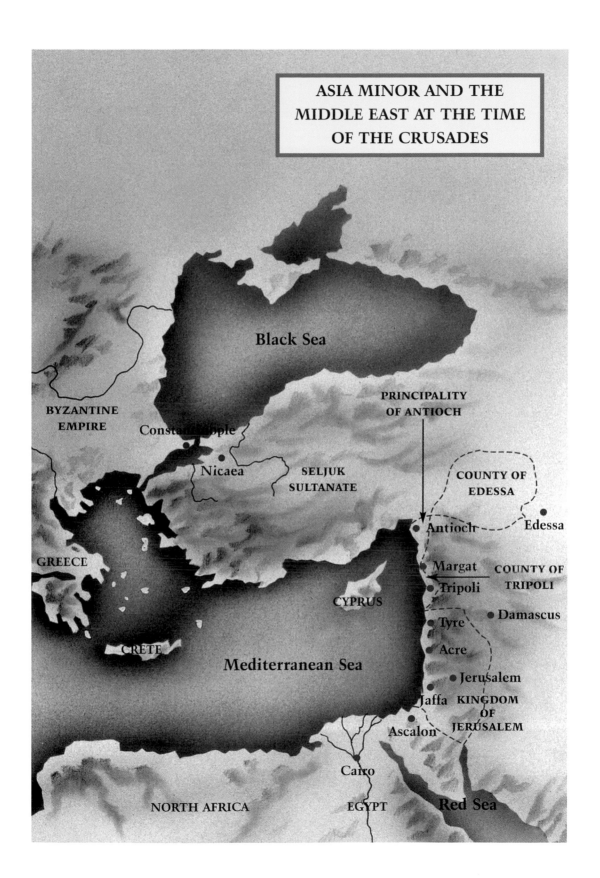

ASIA MINOR AND THE
MIDDLE EAST AT THE TIME
OF THE CRUSADES

Black Sea

BYZANTINE
EMPIRE

Constantinople

Nicaea

SELJUK
SULTANATE

PRINCIPALITY
OF ANTIOCH

COUNTY OF
EDESSA

Antioch

Edessa

GREECE

Margat

COUNTY OF
TRIPOLI

Tripoli

CYPRUS

Damascus

Tyre

CRETE

Acre

Mediterranean Sea

Jerusalem

Jaffa

KINGDOM
OF
JERUSALEM

Ascalon

Cairo

NORTH AFRICA

EGYPT

Red Sea

The Kurdish general Salah al-Din, better known to the crusaders as Saladin, became vizier of Egypt in AD 1169 and eventually united all the Muslims of Egypt and Syria under his rule.

Saladin

aladin was born in 1138 in Tikrit, Mesopotamia, which is now modern-day Iraq. His real name was Salah al-Din Yusuf ibn Ayyub. Salah al-Din was an honorary title that translates as "Righteousness of the Faith." His actual name was Yusuf, and as his father's name was Ayyub, the next part of his name means "Yusuf, son of Ayyub." The Muslims called him by the first part of his name, Salah al-Din, but he was known to the West as Saladin. He was part of the Rawadiya clan, who were Kurds, a group that was hated by the Turks and the Arabs. Despite this, in his later career Saladin would keep faith with his people, and many of the officers and advisors in his army were Kurds.

His father, Ayyub, and his uncle, Shirkuh, were both generals in the army of Zengi, the Muslim leader who had captured the County of Edessa from the crusaders in 1144. When Zengi died in 1146, Saladin moved with his father and uncle to Damascus in Syria, the main city of Zengi's empire. Zengi's son, Nur-ad-din, had taken over Damascus after his father's death, and

Saladin began work for Nur-ad-din, just like his father and uncle had done.

Damascus was known at the time as the center of Islamic learning and teaching, so Saladin received an excellent education. As a boy, Saladin was said to be quiet and very fond of his studies, especially reading books about his religion. But some think that although he enjoyed studying Islam, he wasn't yet as devout a Muslim as he would be in later life. Between 1157 and 1161, his father and his uncle arranged three visits to Mecca. Every Muslim is supposed to make a journey to Mecca at least once in his or her lifetime if able to do so. This pilgrimage, or *hajj*, as the Muslims call it, is an important part of the Islamic faith, but for some reason Saladin decided not to visit Mecca.

His first job was as deputy to his uncle, Shirkuh, the leader of the army in Damascus. In 1164, Nur-ad-din sent Shirkuh and Saladin to Egypt to aid the rulers of Egypt, the Fatimids, in their battle against the crusaders. By 1169, they had beaten the crusaders and entered the city of Cairo, where Shirkuh was made the vizier (prime minister) of Egypt. But within only three months Shirkuh had died, so on March 2, 1169, Saladin took over his uncle's position as commander of the Syrian army and vizier of Egypt.

According to Saladin's friend, Baha' al-Din ibn Shaddad, when Saladin was made vizier he decided to become a more devout Muslim. In thanks for the blessings he believed his god had given him, he gave up a lot of what were considered to be un-Islamic pleasures, such as the drinking of wine. Up until this point, as we saw with his failure to go to Mecca, he had not been a strict Muslim, enjoying as he did such

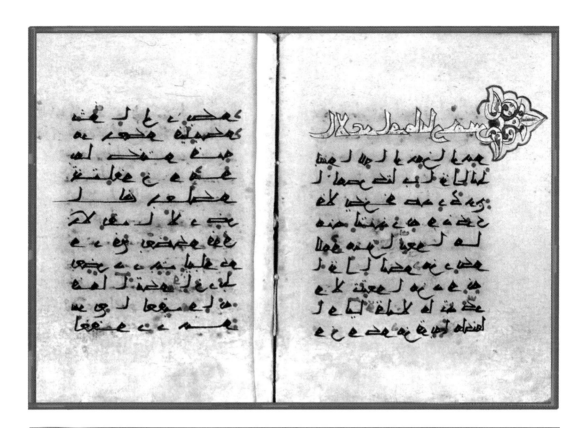

Pages from a tenth- or eleventh-century edition of the Koran, the sacred teachings of Allah as revealed to his prophet Muhammad

activities as hunting and playing polo. But with his new powers, Saladin thought that he should give up such pastimes and concentrate more on his duty to God.

Saladin and his uncle had gone to Egypt to help the Fatimids. But Saladin was an ambitious man who wanted the entire Muslim world to unite against the crusaders. He saw his position in Egypt as the perfect way of building up a power base through which he could become the leader of all the Muslims. The Fatimids were still officially the rulers of Egypt. Even as vizier, if Saladin wanted to take full control over Egypt, the Fatimids would have to be removed from power.

Saladin could simply have massacred the Fatimids and taken Egypt by force. But unlike many of the people in the era of the Crusades, Saladin was not an overly cruel or bloodthirsty ruler. As we will see later, even his enemies, the crusaders, came to respect him for his mercy and fairness in war. The Fatimids had been very corrupt leaders and had built many beautiful and expensive palaces in the city of Cairo, almost turning it into an exclusive area for them-selves, with the general population of the city being forced to live outside the city walls. After the death of the Fatimid leader, the caliph, Saladin expelled eighteen thousand of the Fatimids from Cairo and opened the gates of the city and allowed the population to return and live within the city walls. Most leaders would have seized all of the city's riches for themselves, but Saladin took none of the Fatimids' wealth for himself and refused to live in the luxurious palaces that the Fatimids had built.

The Fatimids had been Shiite Muslims, which was a different form of Islam from Sunni Islam, the one that Saladin believed in. Therefore, he decided to make Egypt conform to his brand of the Islamic faith. To do this, Saladin ordered that the name of the caliph, who was a Shiite, be dropped from the Friday prayers. With the caliph's name left out of the prayers in this way, he had been officially deposed as leader of Egypt. With the caliph out of the way and the Fatimids gone from the city, Saladin could now remodel Egypt for his desired purposes. He wanted not only a strong

A ship in the Persian Gulf, from a thirteenth-century Arabian manuscript illumination

military base, but a cultural center from which he could start building a united Islamic world and an army that could take on the might of the invading crusaders.

Now that Egypt was secured, Saladin turned his attention to Syria and to deposing his master, Nur-ad-din. Saladin's master was becoming wary of him, and he was in the process of taking steps to move against his brilliant and ambitious deputy. But before any action could be taken, Nur-ad-din died in 1174. With his main opponent out of the way, Saladin could now build on the successes he had gained in Egypt. With Nur-ad-din's death, he proclaimed himself sultan of Egypt and called his new regime the Ayyubid dynasty in honor of his father. He quickly expanded his power base. He took over Damascus in 1174, conquered the important city of Aleppo in 1183, and in 1186, captured Mosul.

With these victories, Saladin took vast areas of land from rival Muslim rulers and without doubt became the world's leading Islamic warrior. Despite his overwhelming success, he didn't have it all his own way. The Assassin tribe from the mountainous regions of Syria made two attempts on Saladin's life. The Assassins were a group of fanatical "hit men" who hired themselves out. It is from them that we get our word "assassin." The first attempt on Saladin's life was unsuccessful, but in their second attempt they managed to wound him. In response, Saladin mounted a siege of the Assassin leader's fortress at Masyaf. After three weeks of laying siege to Masyaf, Saladin withdrew his army and never again tried to attack the Assassins. According to legend, it was said that the Assassins had threatened to murder Saladin's entire family if he would not leave them in peace.

Despite his failure to conquer the Assassins, Saladin now had in his possession numerous Muslim armies that were all united under his leadership. His dream had been realized. He had a strong and mighty army that could now join together to fulfill his real aim, the expulsion of the crusaders. Saladin's eyes began to look toward Jerusalem.

The Horns of Hattin, a group of hills south of the city of Acre, where Saladin defeated the crusader army in AD 1187. The victory ensured his capture of the city of Jerusalem.

The Recapture of Jerusalem

Saladin was keen to get the war with the Christians underway, but there was one main stumbling block. In 1183, he had signed a truce with the leader of the Christians, Guy of Lusignan. As was shown in Egypt, Saladin was an honorable man, and although he wanted to get the war started, he was a man of his word and felt bound by the truce. Luckily for him, and unluckily for the crusaders, the truce was broken in 1187 by a crusader called Reynald of Chatillon. Reynald attacked a group of Muslims and held them prisoner. Despite being angry at this break in the truce, Saladin felt that he should negotiate with Reynald and keep his side of the truce, instead of attacking the crusader. Rather foolishly, Reynald refused to even meet with Saladin and still refused to release the prisoners even when ordered to do so by his leader, Guy of Lusignan. Saladin now had the excuse he needed to go to war.

On July 1, 1187, Saladin marched his troops to a mountain called the Horn of Hattin. The weather at this time was incredibly hot, and the crusader army that had been sent to defend Jerusalem was hot, exhausted, and thirsty. Seeing the crusaders' distress, Saladin came up with a clever plan to make their situation even worse. He set fire to some nearby dry brush whose smoke quickly made its way into the crusader camp. On July 4, Saladin attacked. Distracted and unable to breathe, the crusaders were quickly defeated.

The victorious Saladin called Guy of Lusignan and the truce breaker Reynald of Chatillon to his tent. He kindly offered water to Guy. But in revenge for breaking the truce, he took a sword and cut off Reynald's head. Saladin believed that Reynald had deserved this punishment, but he was more charitable to the other crusaders. In a move that was typical of the reputation he was earning for his kindness, Saladin assured Guy that none of the other prisoners would be harmed.

With the entire army of the crusaders virtually wiped out, Saladin could now go on to capture the rest of the Latins' land. Within only two months, his army had captured Tiberias, Acre, Nablus, Toron, Jaffa, Sidon, Beirut, Jebail, Ascalon, and Gaza. It was a disaster for the crusaders. The important port of Tyre did, however, manage to escape Saladin's clutches, and this would have important consequences for Saladin in years to come. And of course, Jerusalem still wasn't in his hands, so he now turned his attention to his greatest goal.

Christian Jerusalem had suffered an enormous loss at the Battle of Hattin. The army had almost been destroyed and the city's leader, Guy of Lusignan, was a prisoner of Saladin. But the city's troubles didn't end there. There were desperate shortages of food in the city, since the Battle of

A depiction of the conquest of Jerusalem by the forces of Saladin in AD 1187, from an early fifteenth-century French manuscript

Hattin had occurred at harvest time. With the area now in the enemy's hands, all the crops were lost. All the refugees who flocked to the city to seek shelter from Saladin's army made the shortage of food even worse. Jerusalem was supposed to be able to house thirty thousand people, but after the Battle of Hattin it was said that the city's population swelled to sixty thousand. And most of these people were women or children who couldn't hope to fight against the invading Muslim army.

Saladin and the Kingdom of Jerusalem

By September 20, 1187, Jerusalem was under siege. Saladin first chose the western side of the city for his attack. As we have seen, the western wall of Jerusalem was heavily fortified by the crusaders, who had built the strong citadel there, around the Tower of David. Most of the Latin soldiers that were left in Jerusalem went to this tower to defend the city. While the fighting continued, Saladin looked for a better position from which to attack the Latins. He eventually settled outside the northeastern section of the city, between St. Mary's Postern and the Jehoshaphat Gate. On September 25, Saladin began his new offensive. Saladin made great use of mangonels, large wooden catapults, to bombard the walls and towers of Jerusalem, weakening the city's defenses and driving the Latin defenders away from their positions. While the mangonels wrought their destruction, Saladin sent ten thousand archers to shoot at the wall's defenders. Another ten thousand horsemen, armed with both lances and bows, waited between the Jehoshaphat Gate and St. Stephen's Gate in the north of the city in case the Latins decided to mount an attack on Saladin's army through these gates.

Saladin's soldiers worked hard to breach the wall so that the army could pour through. Given cover by the archers and the mangonels, they finally caused the wall to crumble, making a breach that was said to be approximately ninety-eight feet (thirty meters) in length. The Latins tried in vain to drive away the invading army with arrows and spears, throwing down large stones and even pouring molten lead on the attackers, but once the wall had collapsed the end was in sight for the Latins. Realizing that their cause was hopeless, the city eventually surrendered on October 2, 1187. The Kingdom of Jerusalem was at an end.

The breach in the wall was at the exact same spot where the crusaders themselves had entered the city in 1099. But whereas the crusaders had brutally slaughtered the city's inhabitants, Saladin and his army did not react in the same bloodthirsty manner. Instead of killing his enemies, he allowed them to leave the city unharmed. They did, however, have to pay a ransom to Saladin for their lives. Each male had to pay ten dinars (the dinar was the currency within the city), the women had to pay five dinars, and one dinar had to be paid if a child was to be allowed to leave the city. All those who paid their money within forty days were allowed to leave the city. Anyone who didn't pay would be turned into a slave.

This may sound quite harsh. But we should remember that when the crusaders took Jerusalem, they showed no mercy to the beaten enemy at all. Men, women, and children, even non-Muslims, were simply killed. And although Saladin collected money from the general population so that they could leave the city, he did allow certain sections of society to leave for free. All the old people who didn't have the money to pay the ransom were allowed to leave without paying, as too were many noblewomen of Jerusalem. Saladin also did not destroy any of the Latins' buildings or loot the riches from the homes or churches. In fact, he actually allowed many of those leaving the city to take their riches with them, including gold and silver jewelry and important treasures from the churches. It was said that the amount of treasure taken out by the Latins was valued at 200,000 dinars.

Those who left the city headed in three directions. Some went to the port of Tyre, some went to the County of Tripoli, while the rest set off for Alexandria in Egypt, where they would be put on ships bound for Europe. When the Latins began to leave the city, Saladin gave each group fifty of his officers so that they would be safe on their journeys. It was said that some of the officers gave up their horses so that old Latins could ride instead of having to walk. Many of the Muslim soldiers carried Latin babies in their arms.

In an age that was often brutal and bloodthirsty, Saladin's kindly attitude toward his beaten enemy was unusual. We might think nowadays that such actions were simply the right thing to do, but in the time of the crusaders such mercy was rare. Armies that captured cities that refused to surrender often killed the inhabitants and stole their riches, just like the crusaders had done eighty-eight years earlier. When we look at how Saladin treated the Latins after Jerusalem's capture and remember his charitable acts when he had taken over Egypt, we can see that Saladin was truly an unusually compassionate leader for his time.

Saladin's Jerusalem

Two knights and ten soldiers were placed in every street in Jerusalem to keep order during the takeover. When Saladin's victorious army had secured the city they knew what their first act had to be. The most sacred Islamic monument in Jerusalem was a massive building called Qubbat as-Sakhrah, or the Dome of the Rock. It was built around AD 690. The dome covers the Holy Rock, the place where Muhammad was said to have gone up to Heaven. The rock itself was enormous, measuring about 54 feet (17.7 m) from north to south, 42 feet (13.5 m) from east to west, and 4.5 feet (1.5 m) tall. The crusaders had renamed the monument Templum Domini, or the Temple of Our Lord, and had installed a large cross on top of the Dome of the Rock. As soon as the Muslims entered Jerusalem, they climbed up to the top of the dome and removed the cross, immediately showing that it was the Muslims who were now in charge and not the Christians.

Saladin had taken Jerusalem on Friday, October 2, 1187. Fridays were of great importance for Muslims, as this was the day of the week when they held their main prayer meetings. Saladin would have liked to have captured Jerusalem early in the day, so that the Muslims could have celebrated their victory during their prayers. But by the time he had captured the city the prayers were finished, so Saladin was determined that the Dome of the Rock should be restored to its Muslim character by the next Friday's prayer meeting, exactly a week away.

In addition to the dome, the crusaders had altered another Muslim building, the al-Aqsa Mosque, just to the south of the dome. The crusaders called it the Temple of Solomon, and it had been the home of the Knights Templar, one of the groups of warrior monks who had settled in Jerusalem. Changing the two buildings back to the way they had once been was not an easy task. To the west of the mosque, the knights had erected some buildings that included toilets and places to store grain, which now needed to be cleared away. The columns and all the other changes made by the crusaders were removed. In place of

The city of Jerusalem showing one of the old walls and the Dome of the Rock, the place from which Muhammad was believed to have ascended to heaven

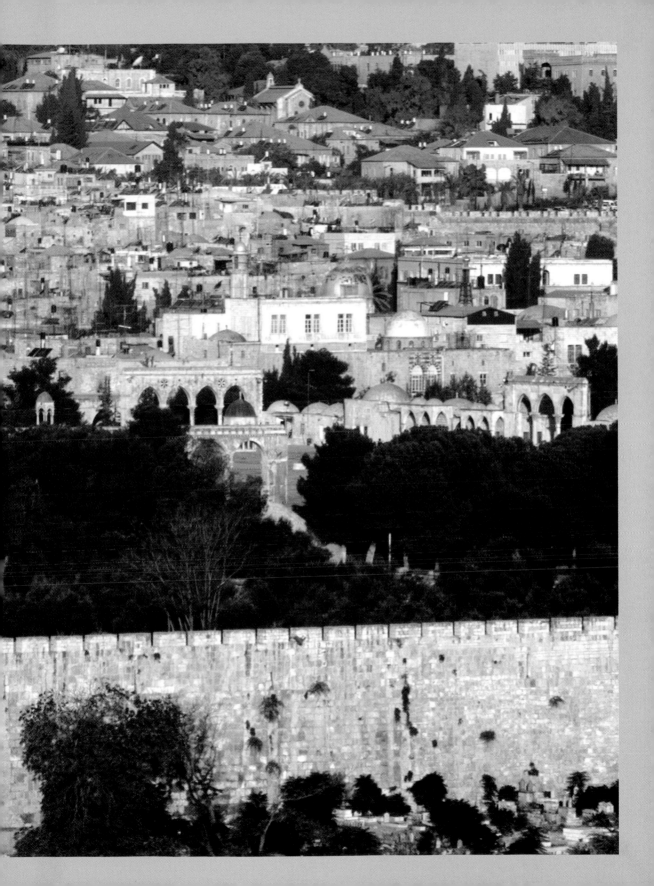

The public library of Hulwan in Baghdad, from a thirteenth-century Arabian manuscript

the straw mats that the crusaders used, Saladin covered the floors with beautiful and precious carpets. He also put up a wonderful wooden pulpit that had been made many years before by his old master, Nur-ad-din.

After Saladin had finished restoring the mosque and the dome, he had them purified with water that had been scented with rose petals, and incense was burned to give the buildings a pleasant smell. It had been hard work, but both the mosque and the dome were now ready for the Friday prayers. In the service held in the al-Aqsa Mosque, the Muslims celebrated their recapture of one of their most holy cities from the Christians. Saladin was hailed as one of the greatest heroes in the history of Islam.

Saladin's rebuilding didn't stop at the mosque and the dome. He transformed part of the Tower of David into a religious building and changed the Church of St. Anne into a school. Many more of the crusaders' churches were reconverted into Muslim mosques. Islam was now the official religion of Jerusalem, but Saladin was not fanatical about forcing his religion on those Christians who decided to stay behind. The crusaders had been part of the Roman Catholic Church, and although these Latin Christians were forced from the city, Saladin allowed other Christians to remain. Before the crusaders had come to Jerusalem, there were various groups of Christians who lived in and around Jerusalem. These native Christians, such as those from the Greek Orthodox Church and the Christians from Syria, wanted to stay in the city that they regarded as their home.

Saladin allowed the native Christians to remain in the city although they did have to pay a *jizya*, or special tax, to do so. At first, Saladin ordered the closure of the Church of the Holy Sepulchre, the church built on the spot where Jesus was supposedly buried, that had been restored by the crusaders when they first captured Jerusalem. But the Greek Orthodox Church asked if they could take control of the church, and Saladin agreed. The Latin crusaders had not always been popular with their fellow Christians, and the Greek church particularly disliked them. For some of their members, the Muslim conquest was a welcome change, because with the Latins having left and the Holy Sepulchre in their possession, they were now the most important Christian organization in Jerusalem.

With Jerusalem now totally under his control, Saladin continued his campaign against the weakened crusaders.

Saladin and the Kingdom of Jerusalem

Saladin moved northward into Syria to attack the major ports, which he did with remarkable success. The exception was Tyre, the port that many of the Latins had fled to after the capture of Jerusalem. The leaders of Tyre had only allowed fighting men into the city. This, along with improvements in the city's defense taken after the first siege, now meant that Saladin faced a hard task in trying to capture Tyre. His army encircled the city while his ships blockaded Tyre from the sea. But a swift and brave attack by a small fleet of crusader ships in the harbor managed to defeat Saladin's ships. This loss, with the siege showing no sign of success, caused Saladin to withdraw from Tyre in January 1188.

Preaching to the faithful in a mosque, an illustration from a thirteenth-century Arabian manuscript

After so many victories, Saladin had finally tasted defeat. His troops were weary and in need of rest, so Saladin sent them back to their homes. After giving his troops this much-deserved holiday, Saladin called them back in May and carried on with his campaign. One of the four crusader states, the Principality of Antioch, was at this time led by Bohemond III, who was a weak leader. By September, Saladin had Antioch surrounded. Bohemond arranged a truce with Saladin, saying that if no help came from other Christians within seven months, he would surrender Antioch to him.

Saladin now looked to the many fortresses that the crusaders had built during their time in the Middle East. In November 1188, the fortress of Kerak surrendered after a

A boat on the Euphrates, from a thirteenth-century Arabian manuscript illustration

year of siege because its inhabitants were almost starving to death. Toward the end of the siege, it was said that people were eating their own horses and selling members of their own family into slavery in exchange for food. Another fortress, Montreal, had to endure an even longer siege, but it too eventually had to give in to Saladin's forces.

On December 6, the fortress of Salad surrendered, as did Belvoir on January 5, 1189. The fall of Belvoir completed two years of almost completely successful warfare by Saladin and his army. The Kingdom of Jerusalem was entirely conquered, apart from Tyre and the castle at Belfort. Of the County of Tripoli, only the city of Tripoli, two small castles belonging to the Knights Templar, one tower in Tortosa, and the fortress of Krak des Chevaliers remained in crusader hands. Only Antioch itself and al-Maraqab remained of the Principality of Antioch. Saladin had indeed destroyed the Latin Kingdom of Jerusalem.

This fifteenth-century French manuscript illustration shows the soldiers of King Philip of France boarding ships for the Holy Land during the Third Crusade. Below, the English fleet of King Richard attacks a Saracen warship.

The Return of the Crusaders

With their once proud kingdom now in ruins, it was inevitable that a new horde of crusaders would come to reclaim their lands from the Muslims. On July 4, 1190, two groups of crusaders left Europe bound for the Holy Land. One army was led by Philip II of France, and the other army was led by a man who would become Saladin's most impressive and formidable opponent, King Richard I of England.

Richard and Philip began attacking the city of Acre on June 8, 1191. The leaders of the city eventually surrendered and agreed to a deal with the crusaders, for which they did not ask Saladin's permission. With Acre taken, Richard managed to make Saladin's forces retreat from the town of Arsuf. The crusader forces now marched toward Jerusalem. Tired and weary from their battles, Richard's troops were in desperate need of food. Luckily they managed to capture a train of Muslim wagons full of supplies that was bound for the city. With this food and the other vital military supplies they had taken from the Muslims, they were ready to commence the attack on Jerusalem.

But Saladin had other ideas. He knew that an army couldn't survive without a ready supply of water for its soldiers. So he ordered his men to contaminate every well between Jerusalem and the crusaders. Now, without any water for his army, Richard was forced to retreat from Jerusalem. He managed another victory at Jaffa, but then news came from England that would force him to abandon the Crusade. His brother, John, was making use of Richard's absence to try to take the throne of England for himself. Richard knew that if he was to keep his kingdom, he had to return home.

Richard had to come to some sort of compromise with Saladin. Reluctantly, he started to negotiate with the Muslim leader. The treaty signed on September 2, 1192, called the Peace of Ramla, was a triumph for Saladin. The crusaders kept only a small strip of land along the coast from Tyre to Jaffa. Ascalon, an important spot on the route to Saladin's power base of Egypt, was to be demolished so that neither Muslim nor Christian forces could take control of it. Saladin was to keep all the inland cities, including Jerusalem. He did, however, allow the Christians access to the Church of the Holy Sepulchre. With this agreement signed by Richard, he returned to England and the Third Crusade was at an end. Saladin's victory over the crusaders was finally complete.

In February 1193, Saladin went to meet some Muslim pilgrims in Damascus who were returning from the hajj to Mecca. That evening he began to develop a fever. During the next few days he fell into a coma from which he never awoke. On July 4, 1193, Saladin died. He was buried in

King Richard I of England and Saladin are depicted here in personal combat, from a fourteenth-century English manuscript.

Damascus. Saladin's Ayyubid dynasty, with its base in Egypt, survived until it was overthrown by the Mamluks, a tribe of ex-slaves who toppled Saladin's family in 1250 and became the new leaders of the Muslims.

Even though the First Crusade had been the only Crusade that had been really successful, the wish of the Christians to keep the Holy Land in their possession meant that even more crusaders would come to try to recapture Jerusalem. The Fourth Crusade set out in 1204 but was diverted from Jerusalem and instead captured Constantinople, the capital of the Byzantine Empire. The Fifth Crusade (1217–1221) was directed against Egypt, the main Muslim stronghold, but this too was a failure.

The Sixth Crusade (1228–1229) managed some success when its leader, Holy Roman Emperor Frederick II, secured the partial surrender of Jerusalem. But the Crusade's success wasn't to last as the Muslims later reoccupied the city.

A double-masted ship of the type used by crusaders to traverse the Mediterranean Sea, from a fourteenth-century Italian manuscript

The Seventh Crusade (1248–1254) again attacked Egypt. The Eighth Crusade was launched in 1270 after the Muslims captured Jaffa and Antioch. And the Ninth and last Crusade (1271–1272) landed at Acre but returned home after a truce had been worked out.

In 1289, Tripoli was taken by the Muslims, and in 1291 Acre, the last Latin stronghold, was captured by the Muslims. This victory saw the end of the crusaders in the region. The Holy Land had been lost to the Christians. When you look at all the Crusades and what they actually achieved, it becomes clear that they were mostly a waste of time. From the time when the first crusaders set out in 1096 to the time when the crusaders were finally thrown out of the Holy Land in 1291, all that was really achieved was 195 years of hatred, death, and bloodshed.

The stone effigy of King Richard I from his grave site in France

In an age of such violence and horror, Saladin is notable as a man who was remarkably different from those around him. Throughout his life, Saladin was famous for his virtues, and there are many examples of why he was to become so admired for his kind and noble character. As we have already seen, his treatment of the Fatimids in Egypt and the Latins when he captured Jerusalem demonstrate that he was a merciful and charitable leader. But there are many other stories that tell of Saladin's generous nature.

After he had taken over as ruler of Syria, he captured the city of Aleppo and the great castle at Azaz, places that had remained loyal to Malik as-Salih Ismail, the son of his old master, Nur-ad-din. When the peace treaty had been signed, as-Salih's little sister paid a visit to Saladin's headquarters. He asked her if she would like a gift, and the

A twelfth-century sculpture from the Abbey of Belval, Nancy, in France, portrays a crusader returning home and reuniting with his wife.

young girl replied, "The castle of Azaz." Even though he had just captured the castle from as-Salih, he gave it back to the little girl's brother.

Lady Stephanie of Oultrejourdain was the wife of Reynald of Chatillon, the man who had broken the truce with Saladin in 1187. When she was freed after Jerusalem had been captured, she asked Saladin if her son, Humphrey of Toron, who had been captured at the Battle of Hattin, could be freed. Saladin agreed as long as the fortresses of Kerak and Montreal surrendered. But when Saladin released Humphrey, the castles refused to surrender.

An Arab physician preparing medicine, from a thirteenth-century Muslim manuscript. Their experiences in the Middle East gave the crusaders an appreciation for Arab medicine, new foods, and exotic spices, and changed European tastes forever.

Being disgusted at this, Stephanie sent her son back to Saladin to be his prisoner again. Saladin was so impressed by Stephanie's noble act that he released Humphrey anyway.

When Saladin met King Richard at Jaffa, Richard's army was outnumbered three to one by Saladin's forces. During the battle, the English king fought bravely alongside his men. Saladin watched his enemy with respect and admiration, fighting as he thought a true leader should. When Richard's horse was killed during the battle, Saladin sent two of his own horses over to Richard to replace the one that had died.

In a time of extreme hatred between people of different beliefs, Saladin stands out as a man of honor, compassion, and mercy. He may not necessarily have had the looks of a traditional hero. He was said to be quite short and stout, with a reddish face, and was apparently blind in one eye. But he was a hero in the true sense of the word, not only to his own people, the Muslims, but even to his enemies, the Christians, who respected and admired him. He was a perfect example of the medieval notion of chivalry, the idea that you should be honorable in all your actions and show respect and mercy to your enemies. Saladin had all of these qualities and even today, many centuries after his death, he is still remembered as a great, kind, and honorable leader.

Glossary

Acre   City captured by Richard I of England on July 12, 1191.

al-Aqsa Mosque   Important Muslim mosque in Jerusalem.

Ayyubid   Saladin's dynasty, named after his father.

Church of the Holy Sepulchre   Christian church in Jerusalem built upon the place where Jesus was supposedly buried.

citadel   A large defensive fortress.

crusaders   Christians who went to the Holy Land during the Crusades.

Dome of the Rock   Important Muslim monument in Jerusalem built on the spot where Muhammad is said to have ascended to Heaven.

Fatimids   The rulers of Egypt before Saladin.

hajj   Pilgrimage to Mecca that every Muslim is supposed to make at least once in his or her lifetime if able to do so.

Hattin   Scene of the Battle of Hattin, where Saladin destroyed the crusader army before attacking Jerusalem.

Saladin and the Kingdom of Jerusalem

Hospitallers of St. John   One of the military orders living in Jerusalem.

jihad   Muslim word for "holy war."

jizya   Tax imposed on the native Christians after the capture of Jerusalem.

Knights Templar   Group of warrior monks that lived in Jerusalem.

Kurd   Tribe of Iraqi people to which Saladin belonged.

Latins   Name given to the crusaders who lived in Jerusalem. They were called this because they were members of the Roman Catholic Church and used Latin for their church services.

Mamluks   Tribe of ex-slaves who took over Egypt from Saladin's relatives in 1250.

mangonel   Large wooden catapult used in medieval warfare.

Outremer   French for "across the sea." The new crusader home in the Middle East made up of the four crusader states established after the First Crusade.

patriarch   Leader of the Latin Church in Jerusalem.

Temple of our Lord   Crusader name for the Dome of the Rock.

Tower of David   Large fortified tower at the western wall of Jerusalem.

Teutonic Knights   Military order from Germany that lived in Jerusalem.

Tyre   Important city port near Jerusalem.

vizier   Prime minister of the Fatimids in Egypt.

For More Information

The Columbia University Medieval Guild
602 Philosophy Hall
Columbia University
New York, NY 10027
e-mail: cal36@columbia.edu
Web site: http://www.cc.columbia.edu/cu/medieval

The Dante Society of America
Brandeis University MS 024
P.O. Box 549110
Waltham, MA 02454-9110
e-mail: dsa@dantesociety.org
Web site: http://www.dantesociety.org

International Courtly Literature Society
North American Branch
c/o Ms. Sara Sturm-Maddox
Department of French and Italian
University of Massachusetts at Amherst
Amherst, MA 01003
e-mail: ssmaddox@frital.umass.edu
Web site: http://www-dept.usm.edu/~engdept/icls/
    iclsnab.htm

Medieval Academy of America
1430 Massachusetts Avenue
Cambridge, MA 02138
(617) 491-1622
e-mail: speculum@medievalacademy.org
Web site: http://www.medievalacademy.org/t_bar_2.htm

Rocky Mountain Medieval and Renaissance Association
Department of English Language and Literature
University of Northern Iowa
Cedar Falls, IA 50614-0502
(319) 273-2089
e-mail: jesse.swan@uni.edu
Web site: http://www.uni.edu/~swan/rmmra/rocky.htm

Web Sites

Due to the changing nature of Internet links, the Rosen
Publishing Group, Inc., has developed an online list of
Web sites related to the subject of this book. This site is
updated regularly. Please use this link to access the list:

http://www.rosenlinks.com/lma/sakj

For Further Reading

Cartlidge, Cherese. *The Crusades: Failed Holy Wars*. San Diego: Lucent Books, 2002.

Hatt, Christine. *The Crusades: Christians at War*. New York: Franklin Watts, Inc., 2001.

Jones, Terry. *The Crusades*. London: Penguin, 1999.

Nicolle, David. *The Crusades* (Essential Histories No. 1). Oxford, UK: Osprey, 2001.

Nicolle, David. *Hattin 1187: Saladin's Greatest Victory*. Oxford, UK: Osprey, 1993.

Nicolle, David. *Knights of Outremer 1187–1344 AD* (Osprey Military Warrior Series No. 18). Oxford, UK: Osprey, 1997.

Nicolle, David. *Saladin and the Saracens: Armies of the Middle East 1100–1300* (Men at Arms Series, No. 171). Oxford, UK: Osprey, 1986.

Rice, Chris. *Crusades: The Struggle for the Holy Lands*. New York: DK Publishing, 2001.

Rice, Earle. Life *During the Crusades*. San Diego: Lucent Books, 1998.

Stanley, Diane. *Saladin: Noble Prince of Islam*. New York: Harper Collins, 2002.

Saladin and the Kingdom of Jerusalem

Tate, Georges. *The Crusaders: Warriors of God.* New York: Harry N. Abrams, 1996.

Williams, Paul L. *The Complete Idiots Guide to the Crusades.* New York: Alpha Books, 2001.

Bibliography

Baldwin, M. W., ed. *The First Hundred Years*. Madison, WI: University of Wisconsin Press, 1969.

Hindley, Geoffrey. *Saladin.* London: Constable, 1976.

Newby, P. H. *Saladin in His Time*. London: Phoenix Press, 2001.

Lane-Poole, Stanley. *Saladin and the Fall of Jerusalem.* London: Greenhill Books, 2002.

Prawer, Joshua. *The Crusaders' Kingdom.* London: Phoenix Press, 2001.

Regan, Geoffrey. *Saladin and the Fall of Jerusalem.* London: Croom Helm, 1987.

Reston Jr., James. *Warriors of God: Richard the Lionheart and Saladin in the Third Crusade.* New York: Doubleday Books, 2001.

Runciman, Steven. *A History of the Crusades Vol. II: The Kingdom of Jerusalem.* New York: Cambridge University Press, 1987.

Index

A

Acre, 32, 47, 50
al-Aqsa Mosque, 37–40, 41
Aleppo, 28, 51
Alexius I, 6
Antioch, Principality of, 7, 43, 45, 50
Arabs, 5, 6, 23
Arsuf, 15, 47
Ascalon, 32, 48
Assassin tribe, 28–29
Ayyub, 23, 24, 28
Ayyubid dynasty, 28, 49

B

Baha' al-Din ibn Shaddad, 24
Baldwin I, 17–18
Bohemond III, 43
Byzantine Empire, 6, 12, 49

C

Church of St. Anne, 12, 41
Church of the Holy Sepulchre, 6, 12, 41, 48
Citadel, 13, 34
Constantine IX, 12
Crusades
  First, 6–12, 36, 49
  Second, 20
  Third, 47–48
  Fourth, 49
  Fifth, 49
  Sixth, 49
  Seventh, 50
  Eighth, 50
  Ninth, 50

D

Damascus, 23, 24, 28, 48, 49
Dome of the Rock, 6, 36–37, 40, 41

E

Edessa, County of, 7, 20, 23
Egypt, 24, 25–26, 28, 31, 36, 48, 49, 50, 51

F

Fatimids, 24, 25–26, 51
food, 15–17
France, 5, 6, 7, 9, 12
Frederick II, 49

G

Godfrey of Bouillon, 9–12, 15, 17
Greek Orthodox Church, 41
Guy of Lusignan, 31, 32

H

haji, 24, 48
Hattin, Battle of, 31–33, 52
Holy Land, 5, 6, 18, 47, 49, 50
Humphrey of Toron, 52–53

I

Islam
  in Jerusalem, 5–6, 41
  spread of, 5

J

Jaffa, 15, 32, 48, 50, 53
Jerusalem
  captured by Christians, 7–8, 13,
    35, 37, 41
  captured by Saladin, 34–37,
    40–41, 45, 51
  as Latin Kingdom of Jerusalem,
    8–9, 12–18, 35
  prosperity of, 18–19
  social groups of, 17–18
Jesus, 6, 12, 41
jihad, 19

K

Kerak fortress, 43, 52
knights, orders of, 18, 37, 45
Knights Templar, 18, 37, 45

M

Malik as-Salih Ismail, 51–52
Mamluks, 49
Mecca, 24, 48
Montreal fortress, 45, 52
Muhammad, 5, 6, 36

N

Nur-ad-din, 23–24, 28, 40, 51

P

Peace of Ramla, 48
Philip II, 47
pilgrimages, 6, 13, 24, 48

R

Reynald of Chatillon, 31, 32, 52
Richard I, 47–48, 53–54
Roman Catholic Church, 8–9, 18, 41

S

Saladin
  capturing Jerusalem, 34–37,
    40–41, 45
  death of, 48–49
  life of, 23–29, 51–54
  as a Muslim, 24–25, 26, 28
  uniting Muslims, 25, 28, 29
  at war against Christians, 31–35,
    41–45, 48
Shiite Muslims, 26
Shirkuh, 23, 24, 25
Stephanie of Oultrejourdain, 52–53
St. Stephen's Gate, 17, 34
Sunni Muslims, 26
Syria, 23, 24, 28, 41, 42, 51

T

Temple of Our Lord, 37
Temple of Solomon, 37
Tower of David, 13, 34, 41
Tripoli, County of, 7, 36, 45, 50
Turks, 6, 19, 23
Tyre, 32, 36, 42, 45, 48

U

Urban II, 5, 6

Z

Zengi, 19–20, 23

About the Author

Lee G. Hancock studied at the University of Gloucestershire in England, where he achieved an honors degree in history and religious studies. He has a lifelong passion for history, especially the Tudor period, Nazi Germany, the Middle Ages, and Soviet Russia. He enjoys reading, playing the guitar, and writing. He lives in Worcester with his girlfriend, Donna.

Photo Credits

Cover, pp. 9, 16, 27, 33, 40, 42, 43, 44, 46, 53 © AKG London; p. 4 © The Bridgeman Art Library; p. 7 © Museo Camillo Leone Vercelli/Dagli Orti/The Art Archive; pp. 10–11, 30, 38–39 © Sonia Halliday Photographs; p. 14 © Uppsala University Library Sweden/Dagli Orti/ The Art Archive; pp. 19, 25 © Christie's Images Ltd.; p. 22 © British Library, London; p. 49 © British Museum/ The Art Archive; p. 50 © Museo de la Torre del Oro Seville/Dagli Orti/The Art Archive; pp. 51, 52 © Erich Lessing/AKG London.

Designer: Nelson Sà; **Editor:** Jake Goldberg;
Photo Researcher: Elizabeth Loving